My Farm, My Heart
Childhood Memories

Me, Cousin Janet, and Desta

Dick

My mom and dad

Dick and Me

Dedicated with love to the Losekes,
Buettners, and all our family who have
come before us, spent time with us,
and those who are our future.

My Farm, My Heart
Childhood Memories

Author
Donna (Buettner) Finn

Writer
Deena (Finn) Meyer

Illustrator
Christine Anderson

Independently published
Copyright (c) Deena Meyer 2021
ISBN: 9798579781819

Introduction

The story of how my family ended up on a farm in Nebraska starts in 1858 when my mother's grandparents *immigrated* from Germany to the United States. Hoping to find a better life in the United States, my great grandparents boarded a large sailboat with hundreds of other Germans. After six long weeks sailing across the Atlantic Ocean, they arrived at Castle Garden in New York.

They provided their paperwork at the immigration center and entered the United States. Next, they boarded a train with all their belongings and headed west. After six days and nights on the train, they reached the end of the railroad tracks in Iowa. From there they traveled in a wagon pulled by oxen. They took turns riding and walking for 350 miles, which took three weeks, and finally arrived in Nebraska, where they would start their new lives.

My great-grandparents chose to live in Nebraska because they wanted to be close to the only family they had in the United States; my great uncle had settled in Nebraska two years earlier. The land where they chose to live was fertile, which meant it was good for growing crops, and it reminded them of the land they had farmed in Germany. Moving to Nebraska was exciting for them because for the first time they had the opportunity to own their land. In Germany, only the wealthiest people owned land.

Through the years, my great-grandparents had children and grandchildren. And as their children and grandchildren grew up, most of them chose to continue living on nearby farms. My mom's family stayed close to her grandparents. When my parents met and got married, they bought a farm that was close to where my great-grandparents and grand-parents had settled. This farm near Madison, Nebraska is where my childhood memories begin.

My name is Donna. I was born in 1938. I grew up on a farm with my parents, Ida and Elmer Buettner. I had 2 brothers: Durwin was seven years older than me and Dick was nine years younger than me. And I have one sister, Desta, who is 2 years younger than me and my best friend. Our farm was located a few miles outside the small town of Madison, Nebraska.

My family

4

Me and Desta

Growing up, my aunts, uncles, and cousins would gather at my Grandma Loseke's farm on Sundays. Everyone brought food to share. My grandma made the best chocolate cake. My cousins and I would poke holes in the top with our fingers and pour milk into the holes to make the cake taste really moist.

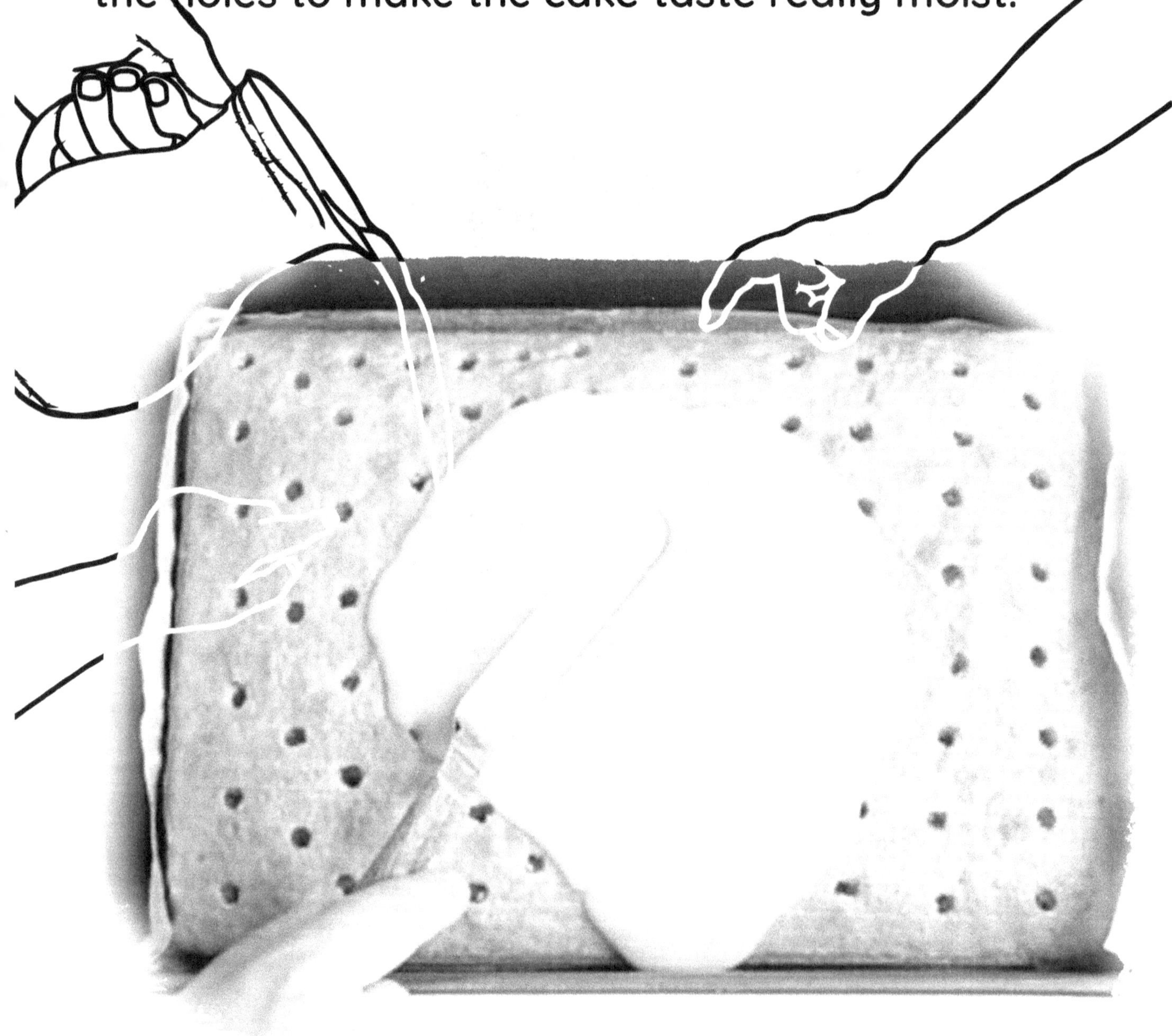

6

My brothers, sister, and I would bring clothes we had outgrown to exchange with our cousins. I couldn't wait to get my older cousin's *hand-me-downs* because I thought she had the cutest dresses.

My grandma spoke German and she would teach us songs in German. One of my favorite songs was "A,B,C, the cat ran in the snow." We didn't hear German spoken anywhere else and I didn't ever learn to speak German very well, but I loved singing the songs with my Grandma.

English translation:
>
> ABC the cat ran in the snow.
> Then she came out again.
> She had white boots on.
> Oh, my! Oh, my!
> The can ran in the snow.

Occasionally my parents let me spend the weekend at my Grandma's. During one of those weekends, my grandma sewed a dress for me. I had picked out a chicken feed sack with a pretty pattern at the general store. I waited patiently for the baby chickens to eat all the food. When the sack was empty, my Grandma used it to make my dress. I felt so special in my new dress.

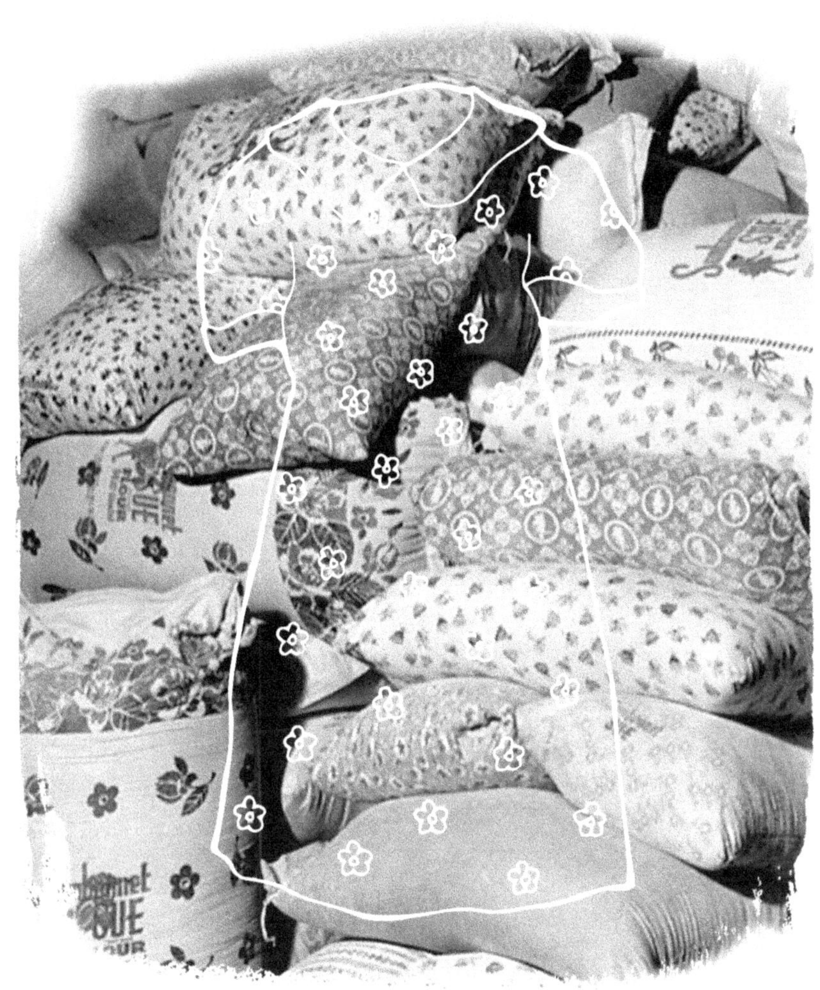

My parents gave each of us *chores* to do on our farm. My sister and I did most of our chores together. One of our chores was to feed the chickens every morning and night.

10

We also collected eggs the chickens laid. Sometimes the chickens did not want to move off their nests and we had to lift them up with a long stick to grab the eggs! At times being in the chicken coop with all the chickens was a little scary, but I knew all the chores we did helped our family.

11

Our family raised horses, cows, sheep, pigs, geese, and chickens on our farm. At various times through-out the year, my dad would sell some of the animals in town where they processed and packaged the meat for us.

12

Our family would store some of the packaged meat in a freezer we rented in town so we could use it for family meals over the next few weeks or months.

13

Our horses helped with some of the hard work on the farm. During *harvest*, they pulled the plough through the field and they would pull the big wooden wagons filled with crops.

I remember helping my dad *shear* the sheep so he could sell the wool. He cut the tails off the baby sheep and my mom used them for dusting. She used geese wings for feather dusters, too. Our geese would chase me and my sister and bite us if they caught us. I did not like our geese!

sheep and geese

15

My dad milked our cows twice each day. He would bring eight cows at a time into our barn and put them into the *stanchions* so they could eat and drink while he milked them.

cows in stanchion

My mom, my sister, and I carried the milk from the barn into our cellar in heavy metal cans. In the cellar, we poured the milk into a *separator* which spun the milk to separate the cream from the milk. We kept some of the milk for our family. My mom used the cream to make butter. I remember how good the butter tasted on my mom's homemade bread. My mom sold the rest of the butter in town.

cream separator

milk cans

butter

My dad planted a lot of corn on our farm. In the fall, when the corn was harvested, we used some of it to feed the cows, pigs, and sheep. We saved some of the corn to feed the animals in the winter. The rest was sold at the *grain elevator* in town.

The grain elevator was right next to the train track. The corn was loaded onto the trains to be delivered to other cities around the country for people to feed their animals. I remember feeling proud knowing the crops we grew on our farm would be used to help feed animals all over the country.

My dad

18

We also grew wheat on our farm. When it was time to harvest the wheat, the nearby farm neighbors would gather at one farm and the men would work in the field and the women would cook for every-one.

After the harvesting was done at one farm, everyone would move on to the next farm until all the neighbor's farms were done. When we were old enough, my sister and I helped with the cook-ing. Everyone was so kind and helpful to each other.

My brothers

The men in the field harvested the wheat and gathered it into bundles. They placed the bundles into stacks called a *shock*. Days later a group of workers that my dad hired would come to our farm and use a *threshing machine* to cut up the wheat and separate the stem from the head, where the grains were found. Similar to how we sold our corn, the wheat grain was sold at the grain elevator and shipped by train around the country for companies to use to make various food products.

wheat shocks

20

After threshing was done, my dad and the workers loaded all the wheat stems into big stacks which were loaded onto horse-drawn wagons and taken into our barn. The wheat stems, or straw, were used for bedding for the animals, especially in the cold winters, and when baby animals were born.

My mom had a big garden in the back of our house. She grew all kinds of vegetables: lettuce, carrots, onions, cucumbers, beans, zucchini, and eggplant. We also had a lot of fruit trees: apple, cherry, and mulberry. When the vegetables and fruits were ripe, my sister and I helped my mom pick them. A lot of times, we ate the fruit and vegetables as we were picking them - they tasted so fresh!

After we picked the fruit and vegetables, we helped our mom save some of them so we could eat them in the winter when they didn't grow on our farm. First, we would boil the fruit and vegetables, then we would pour them into glass jars, and finally we would store the jars in a cool place. Sometimes we stored them in our under-ground cellar, which is like a basement, and other times we'd store them in a cave that was on our land. During the winter, we would eat the food from the jars. It was a real treat!

In addition to storing food for the winter, we also used our cellar for safety from storms, especially tornadoes. From the outside, the cellar had a big wooden door that opened to a stairway made of cement steps. At the bottom of the stairs was the dirt floor.

The cellar always smelled musty, like wet dirt, and it was always a little chilly. We used *lanterns* for light in the cellar because we didn't have electricity. We would wait for storms to pass over, all huddled together in the cellar.

I remember one year when it was time to harvest the crops, my dad got very sick and was in the hospital.

Our neighbors and their tractors

A group of the neighbor farmers decided to help harvest our crops. They all came to our farm with their tractors and harvested all of our corn and wheat. My mom and dad were so thankful to have such kind neighbors.

27

When I was young, we did not have electricity. When it was dark, we used *kerosene lamps* for light and carried them with us from room to room. Because we did not have a washer or dryer, we washed our clothes by hand using a scrub board and we hung the wet clothes outside to dry. In the winter, we hung the clothes on hangers and dried them near the heat from our wood burning stove. If any clothes needed to be ironed, we had to heat heavy irons on the stove and use the hot irons on the clothes quickly before they cooled down.

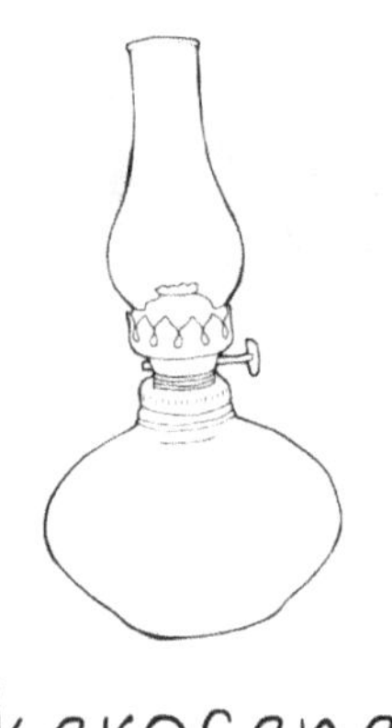

kerosene lamp

wood burning stove

scrub board

We finally got electricity when I was about 10 years old. I remember my dad bought a radio- it was big and made of wood. My dad listened to the farm reports to find out the prices for our crops. My sister and I bought a record player that fit into the back of the radio. My mom ordered records for us and we sat on the sofa and listened to music at night. We really enjoyed the music.

Our water did not come out of a faucet. We had a windmill near the back of our farm. On windy days, the wind blew the windmill and water came up through a pipe to our pump. The water filled up a big round tank for all the animals to drink from. We carried water in big metal pails from the windmill to the house.

windmill

We used the water for cooking, washing dishes, and taking baths. We also carried the water to the garden to water the plants and gave some to the other animals.

My Grannie Buettner at the pump

Because we didn't have electricity, we also didn't have a refrigerator, a telephone, an air conditioner, or heater. Or a bathroom. We had an outhouse.

Our outhouse was a short walk outside the back door. The outhouse was hot in the summers and really cold in the winters. Getting an indoor bathroom when I was 10 years old was one of the best things that happened on the farm.

outhouse

My sister, my older brother, and I would often play in the hayloft in our barn. We would climb up the ladder to the loft where the hay was stored. My dad had carefully tied a big rope onto a beam in the ceiling of the barn. Using a long pole, we would grab the rope and hold on tight as we jumped and swung out into the barn. At just the right time, we let go of the rope and dropped onto the hay-covered floor of the barn. We would laugh as we struggled to get up out of the hay and climb up the ladder to do it again.

Knowing how much we loved swinging, my dad took an old tractor tire and used rope to hang it from one of the big tree limbs by our house. We would swing for hours on nice days.

35

We had a small shed near the house where we stored *coal* that was used to heat the house in the winter. In the summer there wasn't coal in the shed so my sister and I used it as a playhouse. On warm days, it was really hot in the shed and it always smelled like burnt coal ashes, but we loved having our private playhouse.

36

One summer we made our playhouse into a pretend grocery store and another time it was a soda shop. We found thick wheat stems and used them for straws. We made mud pies out of dirt and grass and decorated them with flowers and seeds for our pretend customers.

Tin cans for pretend store

My brothers, sister, and I all went to school in a one-room schoolhouse a few miles from our farm. All the children from the nearby farms who were in 1st through 8th grades attended the one-room country school. We had one teacher for all the children at our school. Several of the children rode their horses to school. There was a barn at the school for the horses.

My one-room schoolhouse

38

After 8th grade, students had to take an exam to qualify for high school, which was in Madison. When my brother Durwin passed the exam, my parents transferred me, my sister, and younger brother to town school and we no longer went to the one-room schoolhouse. It was so nice to be in a room with everyone in my same grade with our own teacher. I still remember some of my favorite teachers, including Miss Owens in 4th grade and Miss Botsch in 5th grade.

My sister and I attended church every Sunday with our Grannie Buettner. We went to Emmanuel Lutheran church in town. After church service, we would go to Sunday school. We dressed in our prettiest dresses for church. Our Sunday school put on Christmas and Easter plays for everyone's families. When I was a teenager, I received the *Rite of Confirmation*. The next year, I taught Sunday school.

Desta, Dick, and me at Easter

40

My sister and I spent a lot of time with our Grannie at her house in Madison. She taught us how to garden, cook, and sew. She also talked with us about how to be a good person. We learned a lot from our Grannie.

My Grannie with grandkids & greatgrandkids

41

Stores in Madison were open late on Saturday nights so people could do their grocery shopping. Sometimes my parents would give my sister and me a nickel or a dime and we would buy paper dolls at the *five-and-dime store* with our money. When we got home, we would have so much fun cutting out the clothes and playing with them.

When I was about 10 years old, a theatre opened in Madison. When my parents went shopping, my sister and I went to movies at the new theatre. The movies were in black and white. I recall seeing a Tarzan movie and several western movies including Roy Rogers, Hopalong Cassidy, and The Lone Ranger. We would enjoy popcorn at the movies. After the movie, we'd meet our parents and drive back to the farm.

Me with my friends in downtown Madison

Occasionally when we were in town, my sister and I would go to our Aunt Margie and Uncle Chalk's home to visit and play cards with them. I remember my aunt became infected with *tuberculosis* and went to stay in the *sanitorium* in Kearney.

People brought her pretty porcelain shoes as good well wishes and she kept collecting them throughout her life. When she was better and back in Madison, my sister and I would clean her glass curio and arrange the shoes for her.

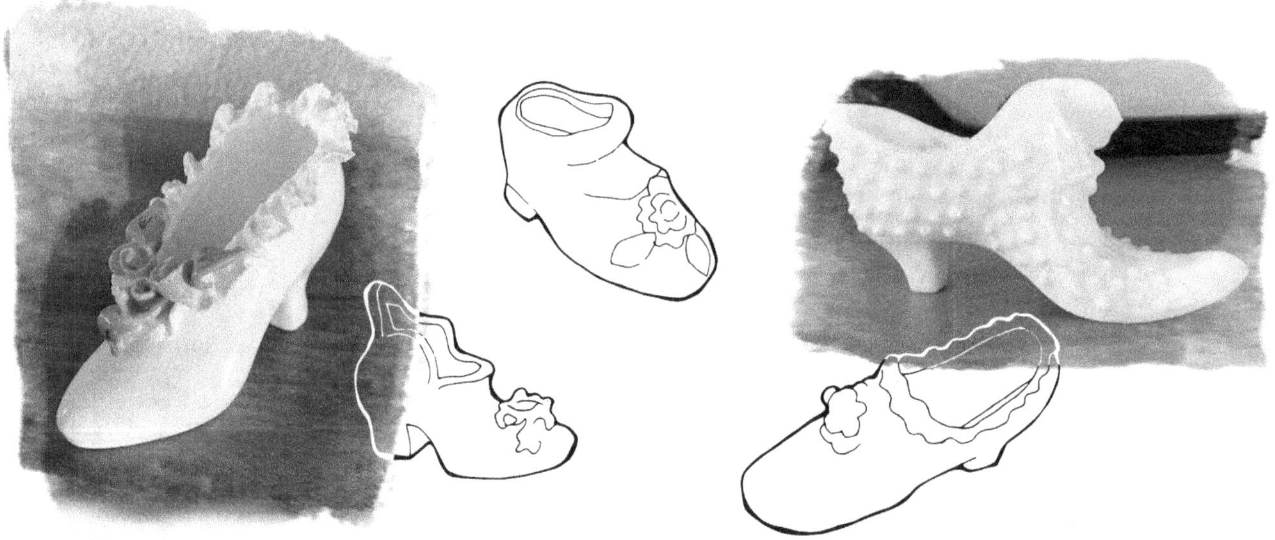

I enjoyed spending time in town. I remember we thought Madison was such a big city. There were about 500 people living in Madison at the time. My sister and I loved going to town to attend holiday parades and sporting events.

44

I went to Madison High from 9th through 12th grade. During high school, I worked in town at the hardware store, selling kitchen *appliances* and tools. My senior year I was a cheerleader and I sang in the chorus.

Me

Me and the
Senior Cheerleaders

After I graduated from high school, I moved away from our farm to go to college. I became a teacher and taught at a one-room school. After teaching a few years, I got married and moved away from Madison and had 4 children. We visited my mom on her farm and my children loved running through the apple orchard, swinging in the tire swing, and play-ing with Tippy, my brother's dog.

My children

46

I now live in Arizona near my two daughters. I have 9 grandchildren and one great-granddaughter (so far). A few years ago, Desta and I visited Madison with my daughter, Deena. We drove by our old farm, watched a parade in town, went to church at Emmanuel Lutheran, and visited with friends from high school. It all looks quite different from what I remember, but my heart still felt it was "home."

Our old farm (2017)

GLOSSARY

appliance. Equipment, usually electric, for use in the home for performing domestic chores, as a toaster or blender.

chore. The everyday work around a house or farm.

coal. Black or dark-brown rock found mainly underground and used as fuel.

rite of confirmation. The act of a baptized person affirming their Christian belief.

five-and-dime store. A store that sold many different items, most of which cost five or ten cents.

grain elevator. A tall building for storing grain that uses a lifting machine to collect and store grain and fill trucks and train cars for shipping the grain.

hand-me-down. Clothing that is passed on to another person after being used or outgrown.

harvest. Gathering of crops or the season when the crops are gathered.

immigrate. To move permanently to a new country.

kerosene lamp. A lighting device that uses kerosene as fuel.

lantern. An old fashion hand-held light.

sanitorium. A special health care facility that treats people with specific diseases.

separator. A hand-powered machine for separating cream from whole milk.

shear. To remove fur or hair by cutting or clipping.

shock. An arrangement of cut-grain-stalks placed to keep the grain heads off the ground.

stanchion. Two or more poles used to keep cattle in a stall.

threshing machine. A farm machine for separating grains from the straw.

tuberculosis. A disease that affects tissues in a body, especially the lungs.

About the author

Donna, the second child of Ida (Loseke) and Elmer Buettner, spent her childhood on the family farm outside of Madison, Nebraska, the setting for this book. Donna has 4 children (Jeff, Julie, Deena, and Scott) who have blessed her with 9 grandchildren (Tyler, Alyssa, Zac, Corey, Morgan, Alex, Brett, Jaysen, and Maiti) and one great-granddaughter (Penelope), with a great-grandson expected in early 2021. Donna spent much of her career in retail store management. Donna now enjoys retirement, residing in Peoria, Arizona. She enjoys visiting with her neighbors, a good basketball, baseball, football, or hockey game, and telling stories from her past.

About the writer

Deena, Donna's 3rd child, was born in Norfolk, Nebraska. Deena spent most of her childhood in Grand Island, Nebraska. After graduating with a Business degree from the University of Nebraska, Deena moved to Arizona. Deena has three children: Alyssa, Morgan (Marshall McKinney), and Brett. She earned her Master's in Elementary Education in 2004 and has worked In the educational publishing industry for the past 13 years. Deena resides in Scottsdale, Arizona.

About the illustrator

Christine Anderson is an illustrator and designer living in Scottsdale, Arizona. More of her work can be found at www.christineandersonillustration.com